bad
cat

by Jim Edgar

with
R. D. Rosen
Harry Prichett
Rob Battles

bad
cat

Hodder & Stoughton
LONDON SYDNEY AUCKLAND

First published in Great Britain in 2005
by arrangement with Workman Publishing Company, Inc., New York

1 2

British Library Cataloguing in Publication Data
A record for this book is available from the British Library

ISBN 0 340 90877 7

Photo editor: John Blum

Printed and bound in Great Britain by CPI Bath

Hodder & Stoughton
A Division of Hodder Headline Ltd
338 Euston Road
London NW1 3BH
www.madaboutbooks.com

to Marlo Menez

Acknowledgments

Jim thanks Alex, his wife
Michelle, his folks, and
Beck Hansen, another chump
from L.A. who made good.

Introduction

It is no secret that Cat owns *you*, and not the other way around. Why fool yourself with delusions of grandeur? Poor human, it's not your fault. Cat has been this way from the beginning, since the Garden of Eden. He gave the paw to Adam and Eve. He surreptitiously controlled the minds of thousands of Egyptians. He usurped Dog's position as household pet for the early Greeks. He has had his paw in the world's business for

millennia. But now Cat has had enough--enough of me, and he certainly has had enough of you.

Subconsciously, you know that inside that lovable ball of fur is a supercilious, sanctimonious, and always underestimated animal. He's not waiting to get out. He *is* out. Only perhaps you haven't noticed as you sit in your hovel littered with old pizza boxes, cigarette butts, and empty fo'ties of Schlitz malt liquor, watching reruns of *Star Trek*, petting the fluffy quadruped you have mistaken for your friend. Perhaps you need more evidence? Perhaps you are unclear about Cat's agenda?

I submit for your disapproval 244 cases in point--244 portraits of felines, their private lives laid bare by a snapshot and a few

lines. See with your own eyes
what Cat is *really* thinking,
although he offers a gentle purr
and a rub against your leg, or
what seems to be a smile in your
direction from across the room.

Want more? Then consult our Web
site, http://www.mycathatesyou.com,
where we reveal the secret
thoughts and urges of thousands
of felines in a terrifyingly
candid fashion. As for the Web
site, and the book you hold in
your hands: Kids, stay away! And
all *Homo sapiens* beware.

That is all.

Jim Edgar

"I call it *fang* shui."

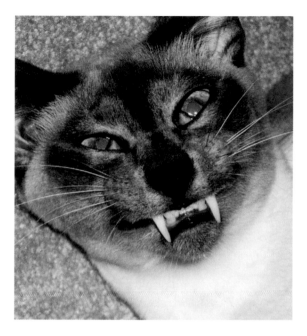

NAME: Bosco
AGE: 4
HOBBY: Breeding carp

"Never mind--it's a joke only frogs and cats would understand."

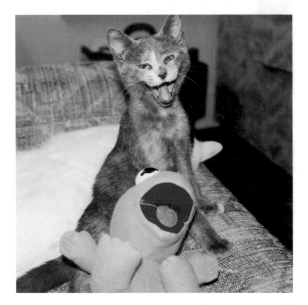

NAME: Peanut
AGE: 1
HOBBY: Internet dating

"The few, the proud, the hairless."

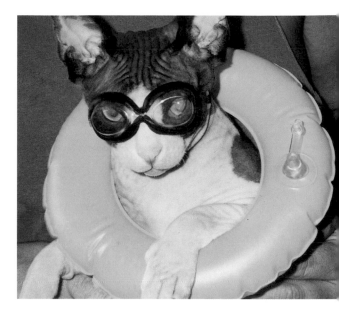

NAME: Jerry
AGE: 6
HOBBY: Racquetball

"Relax--I've done thousands of these procedures."

NAME: Dotty
AGE: 8
HOBBY: Watching *Silence of the Lambs* on DVD

"Take the freakin' picture
already."

NAME: Scooter
AGE: 8 months
HOBBY: Crank calls

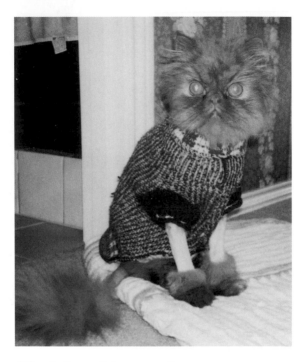

"Chicks dig me."

NAME: Mr. Fliegel
AGE: 7
HOBBY: Collecting Charlie
Parker on vinyl

"I still believe in the research we're doing here."

NAME: Alana
AGE: 12
HOBBY: Reading back issues
of *The New England
Journal of Medicine*

"Soon as the light turns
green, let's see what this
baby can do."

NAME: Chuck
AGE: 8
HOBBY: Collecting Beach Boys
autographs

"She was naked when I
came in."

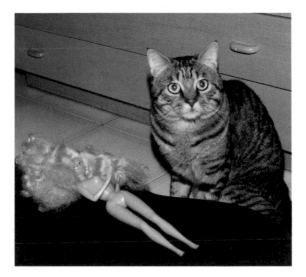

NAME: Clarence
AGE: 5
HOBBY: Frequenting flea
markets

"I think the play date's
over."

NAME: Rosie
AGE: 2
HOBBY: Shopping until
dropping

"Where? Where does it say
'No peeing'?"

NAME: Buckles
AGE: 2 months
HOBBY: None yet

"I assure you lobotomies are making a comeback."

NAME: Brent
AGE: 14
HOBBY: Doubles tennis

"I said no tongue."

NAME: Yvonne
AGE: 6
HOBBY: Trying new bronzers

"I remember when I was the only cat who could juggle."

NAME: Mr. Whiskers
AGE: 15
HOBBY: Collecting Emmett
Kelly memorabilia

"Oh, yeah, baby! Oh, yeah!
I like it like that!!"

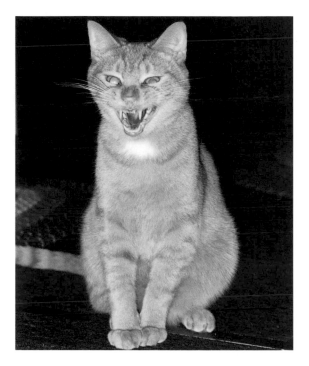

NAME: Garth
AGE: 4
HOBBY: Scrabble

"Jerry Springer called. He wants us next Friday."

NAME: Shanika

AGE: 3

HOBBY: Creating personalized scents

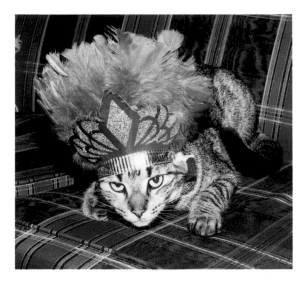

"Take it from me, kid--by
the third show you won't
even know you're naked."

NAME: Terry
AGE: 3
HOBBY: Corresponding with
prisoners

"What the hell is wrong
with you? *Everybody* buys
Girl Scout Cookies."

NAME: Suzy
AGE: 1
HOBBY: Helping little old
Chihuahuas cross the
street

"The only reason I do the pageant is for the free wine."

NAME: Melissa
AGE: 5
HOBBY: Collecting placemats

"If something should happen to me, my son Damian will take over the business."

NAMES: Damian (left) and Falafel
AGES: 1 month, 2 years
HOBBIES: Nursing; darts

"I like to watch."

NAME: Paula
AGE: 14
HOBBY: Popping chondroitin
and glucosamine
supplements

"I've left you this many
surprises in your sock
drawer."

NAME: Rusty
AGE: 3
HOBBY: Amateur magician

"This signal means, 'Start spraying.'"

NAME: Cummerbund
AGE: 1
HOBBY: Internet poker

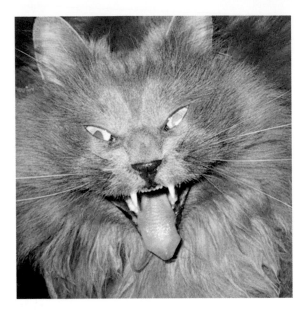

"You never told me you had a sister."

NAME: Alistair

AGE: 4

HOBBY: Cruising kennel corridors

"Look what I downloaded--
and it's free!"

NAME: Maxie
AGE: 1
HOBBY: Instant messaging

"Oh my god!--where are my testicles?"

NAME: Tumbles
AGE: 6 months
HOBBY: Pooping behind the dryer

"I told you the clams were bad."

NAMES: Casimir (left) and Jujube
AGES: 9 months, 4 years
HOBBY: Seafood buffets

"I charge by the
half-hour."

NAME: Wanda
AGE: 3
HOBBY: Watching QVC

"I'm feeling it. Are you feeling it?"

NAME: Larry
AGE: 6
HOBBY: Leaping unexpectedly

"My ball. First down and whatever."

NAME: Wade

AGE: 4

HOBBY: Pencil sharpening

"One step closer and
Sidney's sausage."

NAME: Muncie

AGE: 4

HOBBY: Collecting old *LIFE*
magazines

"Mmmm. Salmon smoothie!"

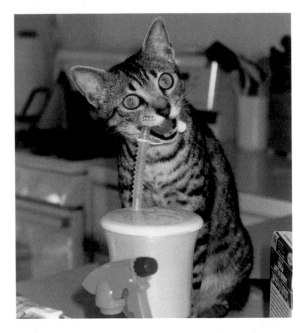

NAME: Foodgie
AGE: 8 months
HOBBY: Watching *Iron Chef*

"I hate playing Operation
with your drunk friends."

NAME: Barbara
AGE: 2
HOBBY: Watching the lawn

"Next round's on me, Stan."

NAME: Penelope
AGE: 10
HOBBY: Eating other cats'
food

"I come from another dimension, in search of mackerel."

NAME: Flek El Danizar
AGE: 1
HOBBY: Moving small objects with his mind

"Now you know why my name is Clog."

NAME: Clog
AGE: 7
HOBBY: Working with sheet metal

"If they fed me more I could spell 'kitty.'"

NAME: Janet
AGE: 2
HOBBY: Buying too much lip gloss

"Have you had your fun
yet?"

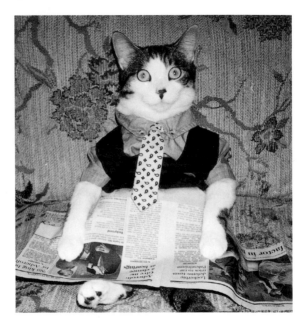

NAME: Gus
AGE: 5
HOBBY: Chasing dust bunnies

"Sonny says you talk too much."

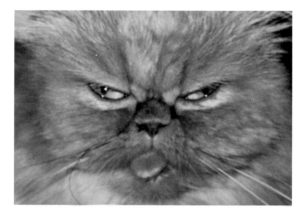

NAME: Anthony
AGE: 17
HOBBY: Bocce ball

"Mrs. Claus told me to meet her here."

NAME: Alfie
AGE: 6
HOBBY: Just get me Mrs. Claus

"Blitzen's a putz."

NAME: Sarah
AGE: 11
HOBBY: Shedding

"Praise the Lord! I've been
weaned!"

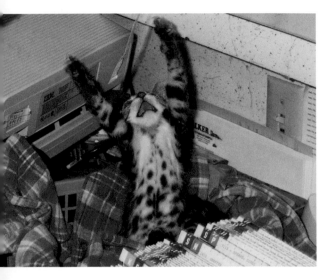

NAME: Niblet
AGE: 12 weeks
HOBBY: Speaking in tongues

"I'll have the burritos and a Corona Light."

NAME: Germaine
AGE: 3
HOBBY: Board games

"I think we're all making good progress, but we have to leave it there until next week."

NAME: Ruth
AGE: 14
HOBBY: Egyptology

"I told you--nobody wants to hear Billy Joel."

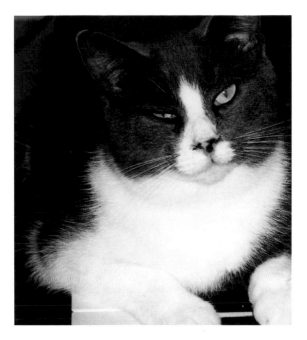

NAME: Stacey
AGE: 10
HOBBY: Compulsive cleaning around the litter box

"Make it look like this."

NAME: Stu
AGE: 8
HOBBY: Drinking the water
in Mexico

"Man, thanks for leaving the Xanax bottle open."

NAME: Creamsicle
AGE: 7
HOBBY: Having staring contests with linoleum

"The first four times I killed it, I swear to God I had no idea it was rubber."

NAME: Appleby
AGE: 1
HOBBY: Browsing through women's magazines

"I found my drink."

NAME: Laverne
AGE: 8
HOBBY: Foosball

"I used to deal catnip to the kittens at the shelter."

NAME: Snax
AGE: 13
HOBBY: Trimming ear hair

"Here's to my recent neutering."

NAME: Algernon
AGE: 1
HOBBY: Bass fishing

"Ten the hard way!"

NAME: Hartley
AGE: 6 weeks
HOBBY: Betting on college sports

"Don't ask, but Klonopin
was involved."

NAME: James
AGE: 2
HOBBY: Taking the metal
detector to the beach

"I don't need to hear about your day. Just open the can."

NAME: Delilah
AGE: 3
HOBBY: Thinking about Abraham Lincoln's hat

"Hey, do I take pictures of you when you're on the pot?"

NAME: Mansfield
AGE: 2
HOBBY: Origami

"Hey, Lou! Mr. High Roller
over here wants to know
where he can find a coupla
broads. Twins."

NAME: Bobby
AGE: 11
HOBBY: Rock climbing

"If you want to call us a cult, that's fine. The spaceship will be here soon."

NAME: Dick
AGE: 10
HOBBY: Neural-linguistic programming

"The gates of Hades swing wide and from the abyss comes Sassafras!"

NAME: Sassafras

AGE: 14

HOBBY: Asking if her ass is too big

"These killing sprees really take it out of me."

NAME: Roland
AGE: 5
HOBBY: Powdered milk fiend

"I would disembowel
you, but what to do with
the eight meters of
intestines?"

NAME: Lady

AGE: 1

HOBBY: Cheech & Chong
movies

"You think I'm cute?
Smell my tail."

NAME: Milo
AGE: 8 weeks
HOBBY: Looking tragic

"Santa told me to tell you
to go to hell."

NAME: Bootsy
AGE: 10
HOBBY: Hating

"Can you tell I've had Botox?"

NAME: Stephanie
AGE: 12
HOBBY: Researching eating disorders

"One bag of catnip, then
I'll let you see the body."

NAME: Klaus
AGE: You're as young as you
feel
HOBBY: Having "accidents" in
the den

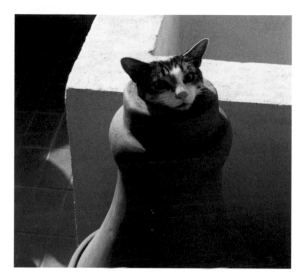

"Don't ever break the law
in Turkey."

NAME: Eric
AGE: 10 months
HOBBY: Customizing
scratching posts

"Got a light, sailor?"

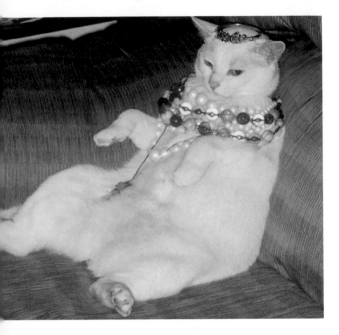

NAME: Fay

AGE: Old enough to know better

HOBBY: What do you have in mind?

"I like a big dumb blonde."

NAME: Mike
AGE: 3
HOBBY: Candlepin bowling

"Harvey, crack me open
another cold one, will ya?"

NAME: Evelyn
AGE: 7
HOBBY: Watching Animal
Plane

"It's hard to say what
fascinates me more, the
drain or my own pathetic
life."

NAME: Ronnie
AGE: 1
HOBBY: Who cares?

"When you're through, I'd like to pee on that."

NAME: Gary

AGE: 9

HOBBY: Racing back and forth in the upstairs hall

"I think the 'shrooms are kickin' in."

NAME: Ravi
AGE: 11
HOBBY: Following The Dead

"There's no card--how do
you know it's for you?"

NAME: Clarissa
AGE: 8
HOBBY: Nipping

"I see kidney failure in
your future."

NAME: Madame Farousha
AGE: 14
HOBBY: Trances

"I lost one to a Doberman and I chewed the other off myself."

NAME: **J.T.**
AGE: **5**
HOBBY: **Attacking strangers' calves**

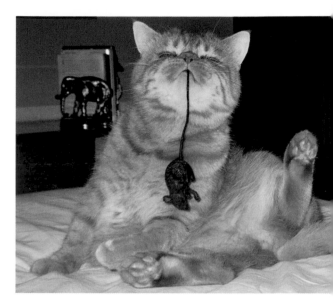

"Mmmm. Blackened Mouse. A Cajun favorite."

NAME: Laura

AGE: 16

HOBBY: Bingeing on Cat Chow

"C'mon--stick your paw in
the socket. I dare ya!"

NAME: Wilson
AGE: 3
HOBBY: Reggae

"You're gonna love this place. Everyone's neutered."

NAMES: Jackie (top) and Flo
AGES: Both 4
HOBBY: Swing dancing

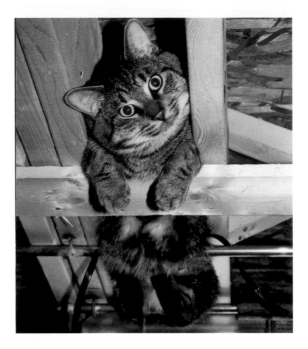

"From up here, I can see cleavage!"

NAME: Elmer
AGE: 2
HOBBY: Stickball

"Of course I believe it's never happened to you before."

NAME: Judy

AGE: 2

HOBBY: Crystal healing

"There was nothing illegal
about that hit."

NAME: Lloyd
AGE: 3
HOBBY: Cheerleaders

"If eating kittens is evil,
then, yes, I'm evil."

NAME: Wilhelmina
AGE: 4
HOBBY: Needlepoint

"It's the hairpiece that gets everyone excited."

NAME: Cliff
AGE: 13
HOBBY: Following the Arena Football League

"After I drink a fo'tie,
I am poppin' a cap in yo
ass!"

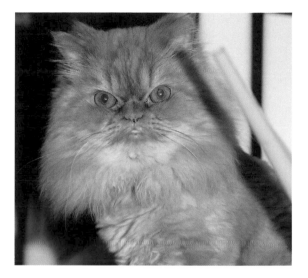

NAME: Norm
AGE: 12
HOBBY: Catfishing

"I have opposable thumbs and I know how to use them."

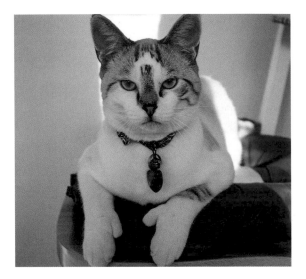

NAME: Hitchcock
AGE: 8
HOBBY: Tracking down his biological father

"I said *shaken*, Miss Galore, not stirred."

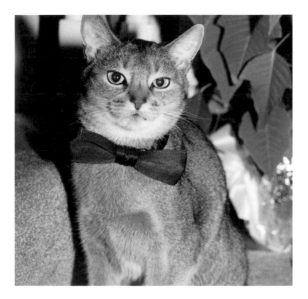

NAME: Otto
AGE: 10
HOBBY: Canoeing

"How many times do I have to say it? No luau."

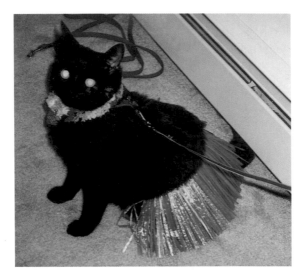

NAME: Megan

AGE: 5

HOBBY: Collecting Fancy Feast labels

"This yoga pose lets me enter your room silently."

NAME: Ashaka
AGE: 7
HOBBY: Cross-stitching

"Remember to go light on
the bleach. I have a date."

NAME: Heddy
AGE: 5
HOBBY: Looking at the Lava
lamp in Sheila's room

"Oh, did I scratch your face? I'm terribly sorry."

NAME: Rikki
AGE: 2
HOBBY: Creating Thanksgiving dioramas

"This is Shelly's and my third booze cruise!"

NAMES: Shelly (left) and Dean Winkler

AGES: Both 1

HOBBY: Bridge

"Like I would know one day
from another."

NAME: Abigail
AGE: 4
HOBBY: Sand art

"Holy crap. Three reincarnations and you're *still* here?"

NAME: Eddie
AGE: 3
HOBBY: Knocking over expensive objets d'art

"Yeah, I'm a half-wit. Who's asking?"

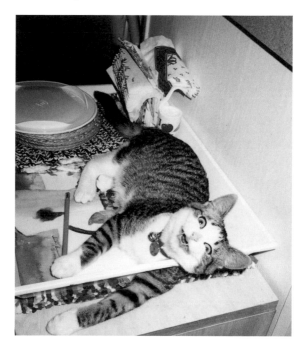

NAME: Doodles
AGE: 3
HOBBY: Humming

"Isn't it ironic that this ancient Shaolin-style move is the last thing you'll see?"

NAME: Cookie
AGE: 1
HOBBY: Casting a spell on the neighbor's dog

"It's amazing what you can
see for twenty-five cents."

NAME: Mickey
AGE: 1
HOBBY: Mortal Kombat

"There was a problem in the teleportation chamber."

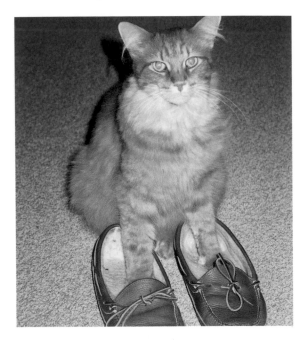

NAME: Anastasia
AGE: 9
HOBBY: Playing soccer with wads of paper

"Something stinks. Okay,
you two--which one?"

NAME: Zanzibar
AGE: 7 months
HOBBY: Lateral leaping

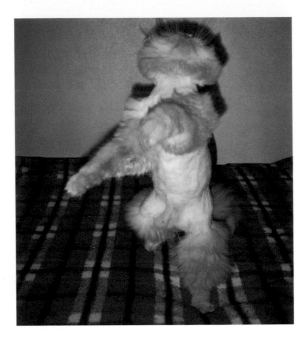

"Damned Ecstasy."

NAME: Macadamia
AGE: 6
HOBBY: Collecting glow
sticks

"I'm not coming out till
Homeland Security tells
me to."

NAME: Serafina
AGE: 4
HOBBY: Soy products

"The water's great, but the chlorine level's a tad high."

NAME: Sharlene
AGE: 11
HOBBY: Organizing kitchen drawers

"Please tell the victims'
families I'm sorry."

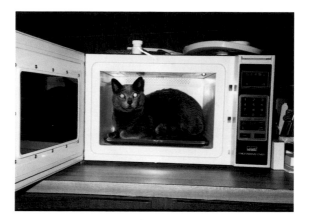

NAME: Smoky
AGE: 9
HOBBY: Making license plates

"Come over here. I want
to show you something
really cool."

NAME: Dorkhead
AGE: 2
HOBBY: Licking dinner
plates

"Philly, hand me the wirecutters."

NAME: Spengler
AGE: 8
HOBBY: Stripping furniture

"Damn--no radio."

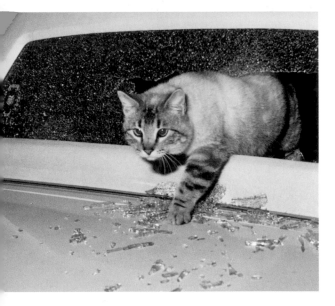

NAME: Spanky
AGE: 5
HOBBY: Rewiring lamps

"When my kitty porn days
are over, I'd like to teach
ballroom dancing."

NAME: Mokey-Mokey
AGE: 2
HOBBY: The Texas two-step

"One word:
haaaaaaaaalitosis!"

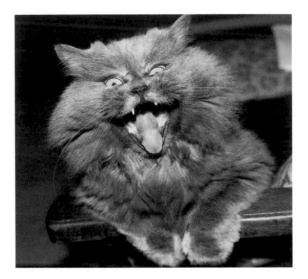

NAME: Monica
AGE: 2
HOBBY: Working in pastels

"Bad cat? No, *Bat Cat*."

NAME: Blanche
AGE: 4
HOBBY: Letting people
humiliate her

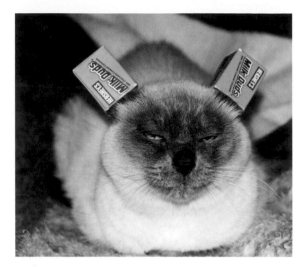

"I'm not listening.
Not listening.
Can't hear you."

NAME: Sashimi
AGE: 9
HOBBY: Pitying the fool who
don't like Mr. T.

"Hey, guys--I found the erotica."

NAME: Bamba
AGE: 1
HOBBY: Getting in the lingerie drawer

"I've never even heard of Krispy Kreme. Look in the car again."

NAME: Lieutenant Feedalot
AGE: 7
HOBBY: Superhero comics

"My master went to the former Soviet Union and all I got was this lousy bust of Yeltsin."

NAME: Katnikov
AGE: 7
HOBBY: Reading Che Guevara

"That's right, Tweety--you
did taw a puddy tat."

NAME: Stanford
AGE: 4
HOBBY: Slide piano

"Yes, officer, I know the routine."

NAME: Ding Dong
AGE: 2
HOBBY: Squatting

"Say that thing about my
hair balls again."

NAME: Janice
AGE: 10
HOBBY: Being a love sponge

"I think I look foxy in a high waist."

NAME: Helene
AGE: 8
HOBBY: Sewing

"Pour some tequila into my
navel and lie to me."

NAME: Lizzy
AGE: Young enough to get
you in trouble
HOBBY: Sex

"That was fun. Now let's try 'whip.'"

NAME: Kevin
AGE: 2
HOBBY: Trying new cheeses

"Tell me you're sorry
again, but say it louder."

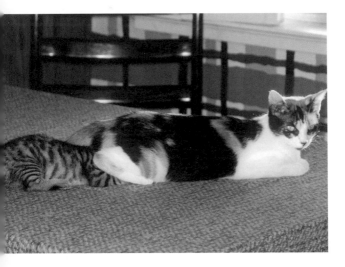

NAMES: Aquarius (left)
and Muddles
AGES: 5 months, 2 years
HOBBIES: The ball with the
little bell inside;
Greco-Roman wrestling

"Stop crying and cuff me."

NAME: Marilyn
AGE: 4
HOBBY: Decoupage

"At my age, it's nice just to cuddle."

NAME: Marmelstein
AGE: 14
HOBBY: Buying in bulk

"Last thing I remember is
the fourth margarita."

NAME: Lucinda
AGE: 1
HOBBY: Urinating

"I don't know, but it has to do with recombinant DNA and a fruit bat."

NAME: Crispy
AGE: 9 weeks
HOBBY: "Drunken-style" kung fu

"Boy, do I love ear!"

NAME: Francine
AGE: 1
HOBBY: Off-season clamming

"Three words: witness . . .
protection . . . program."

NAME: Victor Two-Chins
AGE: 6
HOBBY: Ceramics

"I'm a freak? You built it."

NAME: Misty
AGE: 4
HOBBY: Sleeping in front of
heating ducts

"Wow. I've never seen ones like that before."

NAME: Brian
AGE: 3 months
HOBBY: Hiding in shoes

"Don't move, baby--I want
this lit just right."

NAME: Jerry G.
AGE: 1
HOBBY: Smoking meats

"I think it's time to go
back to rehab."

NAME: Petosky
AGE: 8 months
HOBBY: Eating freedom fries

"Too much gel."

NAME: Myrna
AGE: 1
HOBBY: Daytime soaps

"Actually, I think an all-cat production of *The Crucible* is long overdue."

NAME: Goody
AGE: 2
HOBBY: Playing the zither

"Speak for yourself. I'd still rather do *Guys and Dolls*."

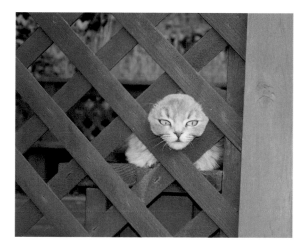

NAME: Armando
AGE: 4
HOBBY: Pooping in the perennials

"I'm clown bait."

NAME: Rhoda
AGE: 4 months
HOBBY: Unicycling

"Ask me nicely or you're
not getting your pants
back."

NAME: Barley
AGE: 2
HOBBY: Wrestling inanimate
objects

"I see what you're doing--
and I like it very much."

NAME: Agnes
AGE: 12
HOBBY: Getting pedicures

"Yes, Your Honor. I do understand the charges."

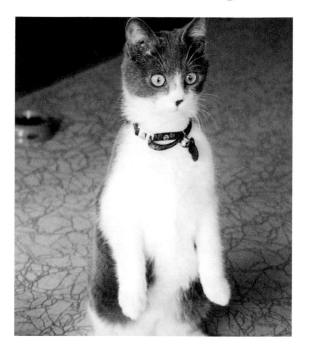

NAME: Buzzy
AGE: 3
HOBBY: Fondue

"Sure I could kill you, but that would be too easy."

NAME: Bartholomew
AGE: 17
HOBBY: Checkers

"The Three Mile Island campground? Right over there."

NAME: Sean
AGE: 9 months
HOBBY: Little League coaching

"I see London, I see France, I can see your underpants--wait--uh oh."

NAME: Klezmer
AGE: 3
HOBBY: Studying geysers

"What can I say?--he's good in bed."

NAME: Ariana

AGE: 4

HOBBY: Checking reflection in store windows

"In prison, I learned many crafts."

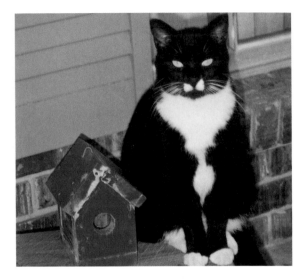

NAME: Happy
AGE: 9
HOBBY: Jailhouse tattooing

"Teddy and I do as we
like, don't we, Teddy?"

NAME: Andrea
AGE: 1
HOBBY: Looking at motorcycle
magazines

"Ken who?"

NAME: Roger
AGE: 3
HOBBY: Sardines

"Forget the donkey show.
Mojitos on the patio!"

NAME: Babs
AGE: 6
HOBBY: Making poi

"All I need now is a
bunker."

NAME: Dwayne
AGE: 5
HOBBY: Ammo

"Hold it right there. Put down the nail clippers nice and slow."

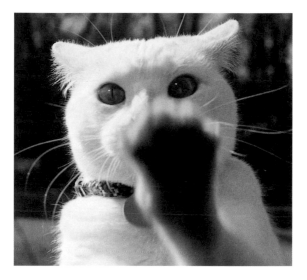

NAME: Gwen
AGE: 2
HOBBY: Using the Jedi mind trick

"This has been fun, but I'm scheduled to be spayed in half an hour."

NAMES: Sally (left) and Ethel
AGES: 4 months, 4 years
HOBBY: Mother-daughter
mah-jongg

"You German Shepherds are
all alike."

NAME: Antonia
AGE: 4
HOBBY: Wearing lederhosen

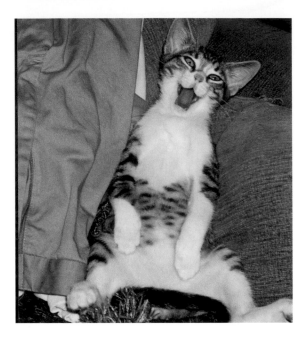

"Now *that's* what I call catnip!"

NAME: Steve
AGE: 8 months
HOBBY: Zoning out

"I know that everything about it is wrong, but I just can't help myself."

NAME: Wyatt
AGE: 12
HOBBY: Pilates

"No matter how often I see it, it still disgusts and excites me."

NAME: General Burnside
AGE: 1
HOBBY: Falsetto hissing

"Touch my doubloons, matey, and I'll batten down your hatches."

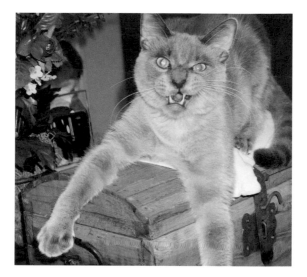

NAME: Cap'n Hairball
AGE: 4
HOBBY: Removing barnacles

"That's it, Fred—that's my
last year working Macy's."

NAMES: Fred (left) and Homer
AGES: 8, 9
HOBBIES: Daytime television;
lighting matches

"It blocks out more than harmful rays. It blocks out you."

NAME: Philippe
AGE: Don't bother me
HOBBY: Not interested

"I know he's passed out,
but his mouth is open."

NAME: Gabby
AGE: 10
HOBBY: Dipping paws in the
fish tank

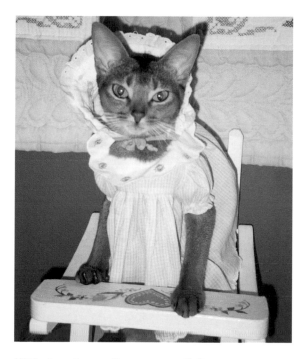

"This has been a blast. Now
change me."

NAME: Doug
AGE: 2
HOBBY: Skeet shooting

"Note to self: stop after third lick."

NAME: Lisa
AGE: 9
HOBBY: Flinching

"We're not laughing with
you. We're laughing *at* you."

NAME: Cardigan
AGE: 7
HOBBY: Frightening small
children

"I vomited on your wallet.
Deal with it."

NAME: Perry
AGE: 1
HOBBY: Eating garbage

"My whole family's
big-boned."

NAME: Raffina
AGE: Middle years
HOBBY: Belly dancing

"Now you sleep with the fishes."

NAME: John "The Valve" O'Brien
AGE: 6
HOBBY: Lawn maintenance

"No more scurrying for you,
mister."

NAME: Felix
AGE: 6
HOBBY: Collecting mouse
heads

"I told you they were easy to install."

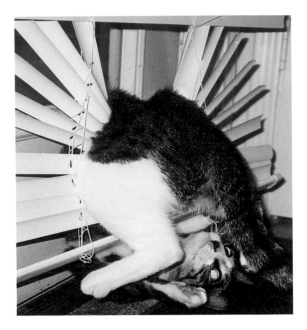

NAME: Lance
AGE: 4
HOBBY: Canning

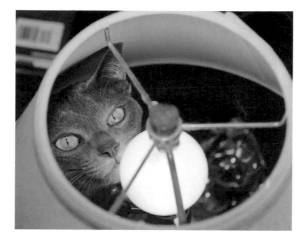

"You will meet a hairless
charmer and bear him six
babies. Your career is
about to take off. Avoid
Scorpios."

NAME: Marcella
AGE: 9
HOBBY: Aromatherapy

"My therapist thought it would be good for my self-esteem."

NAME: Jasmine
AGE: 13
HOBBY: Nail-biting

"I'm sorry, Mrs. Carson, but these are made of plastic. I'll give you a dollar fifty for them."

NAME: Doc
AGE: 9 months
HOBBY: Making citizen's arrests

"Like **you**, this is where I do my best thinking."

NAME: Julius
AGE: 9
HOBBY: Imagining what it's like to be human

"Do *not* try that again. I
eat first, then the ferret,
then you."

NAME: Battista
AGE: 2
HOBBY: Running headlong
into glass doors

"Now, class, a blow to this area will shatter the orbital bone."

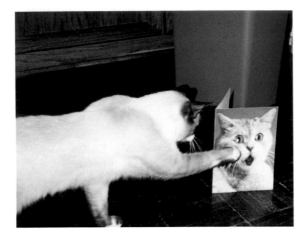

NAME: Raul
AGE: 11
HOBBY: Soldering

"The one thing we miss about the carnival circuit is the drunken midget orgies."

NAMES: Sharon (left) and Karen

AGES: 6, 6

HOBBY: Trying not to breathe on each other

"Yo, yo, yo mutha! Respect this shiznit!"

NAME: D.J. Hummer

AGE: 4

HOBBY: Waiting for the Cubbies to win the pennant

"I have busts made of all my former owners."

NAME: Fiona
AGE: 19
HOBBY: Networking

"Trust me. The plan will work. Shit on the carpet until we get tuna."

NAMES: Madeleine (left) and Drew
AGES: Both 6 weeks
HOBBY: Carpet-soiling

"Smell it. I think I
stepped in dog doo."

NAMES: Louie (left) and
Stewie
AGES: 2, 3
HOBBY: Colonial cooking

"Gentlemen, I give you my masterpiece--a high-pressure meal delivery system."

NAME: Myron
AGE: 10
HOBBY: Shortwave radio

"You're not flossing, are
you, Boozer?"

NAME: Nadine
AGE: 3
HOBBY: Knocking back
jug wine

"I wish I hadn't killed the nice little doll family."

NAME: Chester
AGE: 8
HOBBY: Cop shows

"For my next impression,
I'd like to do a frittata."

NAME: Hector
AGE: 12
HOBBY: Autoharp

"The twins don't say much,
but they're very, very
thorough."

NAME: Svetlana
AGE: 3
HOBBY: Torturing ants

"He who denied it supplied it, but I'll still take a whiff."

NAME: Sebastian
AGE: 5
HOBBY: Flatulence connoisseur

"Just leave *The Watchtower* on the stoop."

NAME: Tangerine
AGE: 4
HOBBY: Vacuuming

"I'm afraid your
grandmother won't
be back."

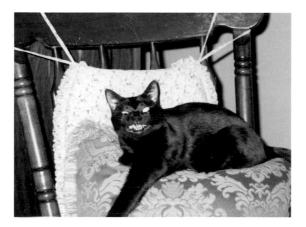

NAME: Dominick
AGE: 4
HOBBY: Taxidermy

"This is my last show."

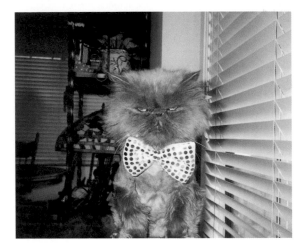

NAME: Mr. Moheb
AGE: 13
HOBBY: Cockfighting

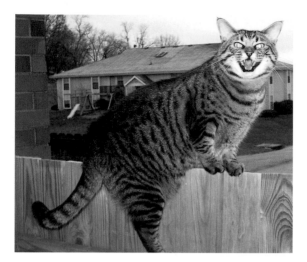

"I'm through with all a
ya--you and ya stinkin',
shallow suburban lives."

NAME: Davis

AGE: 3

HOBBY: Elvis impersonator

"I hate candy. And now I hate you."

NAME: Marvin
AGE: 3
HOBBY: Light opera

"Polly want to get the hell
out of my face?"

NAME: Jennifer
AGE: 6
HOBBY: Anger management

"Listen—the farmer takes a wife, the wife takes you, *you* take the cheese, and leave me out of it."

NAME: Clancy
AGE: 6
HOBBY: Washing left front paw

"C'mon, will ya--I'm on my
break."

NAME: Sarge
AGE: Go away
HOBBY: Beat it

"What winning tickets?
These are mine."

NAME: Tito
AGE: 5
HOBBY: River tubing

"I feel sexy in my tiny sombrero."

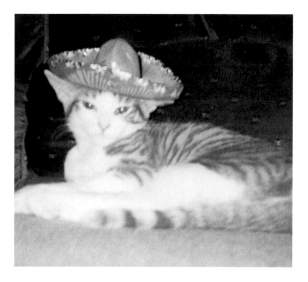

NAME: Mitzi
AGE: 1
HOBBY: Making chili

"See? No canary."

NAME: Boz
AGE: 2
HOBBY: Baroque music

"How's it going down there? You got enough air?"

NAME: Larkin
AGE: 3
HOBBY: Paintball

"Slowly now, and I want it all in crisp tens and twenties."

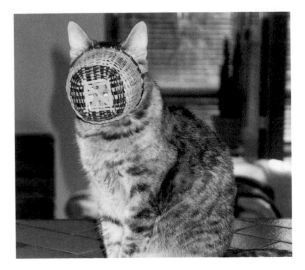

NAME: "Mr. Gray"
AGE: 5
HOBBY: Collecting dried turds

"Not for all the money in
the world."

NAME: Debbie
AGE: 6
HOBBY: Kabbalah

"I sent them to your
ex-wife's lawyer. Why?"

NAME: June
AGE: 8
HOBBY: Balloon animals

"I hate myself for what I now have to do to you."

NAME: Spencer
AGE: 8 weeks
HOBBY: Spearfishing

"I have already written your obituary. It's on the counter."

NAME: Margie
AGE: 1
HOBBY: Puppetry of the ancients

"I'll need a helicopter
out of here and five pounds
of kitty litter."

NAME: Unknown
AGE: Unknown
HOBBY: Not available

"Boo."

NAME: Feldman
AGE: 10
HOBBY: Testing monocles

"You should see me when
I'm wet."

NAME: Seiji
AGE: 2
HOBBY: Biting the people who
did this

"She doesn't care if I come home drunk, and that's all I care about."

NAME: Sugar Pie Honey
AGE: 17
HOBBY: Polishing wax fruit

"Oh, that's choice!"

NAME: Brenda
AGE: 4
HOBBY: Old Peggy Lee
records

"All for one, one for all--
yeah, yeah, just get me
out of this hat."

NAME: Marbles
AGE: 4
HOBBY: Visiting living
history museums

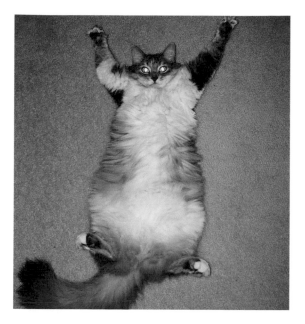

"Don't shoot. Take the
wallet. It's in my left
pocket."

NAME: Cleveland
AGE: 3
HOBBY: Cursing in Spanish

"You guys get the reindeer.
The fat guy's mine."

NAMES: (left to right) Bucky,
Carrot Face, Moe, Irving
AGES: 6, 7, 1, 10
HOBBY: Holiday hijinks

"I smoke--that's why
they're yellow."

NAME: Herman
AGE: 7
HOBBY: Raising cherry
tomatoes

"Put your shirt back on."

NAME: Prince
AGE: 5
HOBBY: Bible study

"I can't wait to get out of
the Hamptons."

NAME: Mitch
AGE: 4
HOBBY: Looking at old issues
of *Maxim*

"It saw me and reared up just like this. It was definitely Sasquatch."

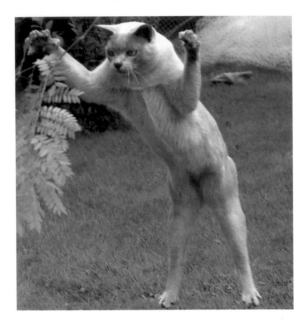

NAME: Andy
AGE: 8
HOBBY: Photoshop

"After this, I'll show
you something really
disgusting."

NAME: Melvin
AGE: 12
HOBBY: Scotch

"I love the smell of dirty underwear."

NAME: Erin
AGE: 2
HOBBY: Smelling dirty
underwear

"That cheating tramp. Give
me a double."

NAME: Arnold
AGE: 5
HOBBY: Monogamy

"Give me some of that good troll lovin'."

NAME: Amanda
AGE: 3
HOBBY: Listening to American musical comedy sound tracks

"I vant to suck your blood."

NAME: Petro
AGE: 12
HOBBY: Hitchhiking

"Good god! Please don't tell me the inside of my mouth looks like that."

NAMES: Marty (left) and Brad
AGES: 1, 4
HOBBY: Texas Hold 'Em poker

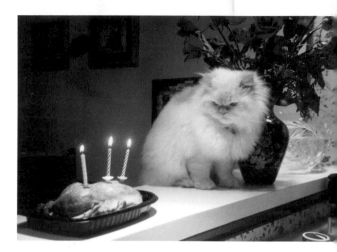

"Strangest damn funeral
I've ever been to."

NAME: Oscar
AGE: 6
HOBBY: Practicing scowl

"Hey, honey! Guess whose new neighbors are nudists?"

NAME: Jim
AGE: 14
HOBBY: Getting funky

"Sorry. Private party."

NAME: Meatloaf
AGE: 15
HOBBY: Nuffin'

"I'm picking up a signal
from Minsk."

NAME: Hermione
AGE: 3
HOBBY: Googling own name

"Could I look any *less* like a cat?"

NAME: Lex
AGE: 4
HOBBY: Old postcards

"I love older women, but
boy am I pooped!"

NAME: Nick

AGE: 4

HOBBY: Octogenarians

"For a can of sardines, I
go both ways."

NAME: Pat
AGE: 2
HOBBY: Welding

"Bye Donner, bye Prancer--
next time bring more of
that excellent North Pole
weed."

NAME: Miranda

AGE: 2

HOBBY: Fantasizing about
fish

"Mom! You're home early!"

NAME: Wicky
AGE: 3
HOBBY: Assault and battery
of upholstery with intent
to shred

"It *smells* like Betsy Ross slept here."

NAME: Shannon
AGE: 5
HOBBY: Social Security check fraud

"Take a whiff and guess what I did."

NAME: Blake
AGE: 9
HOBBY: Playing sock hockey

"Whenever I put the spider on my head, I feel irresistible."

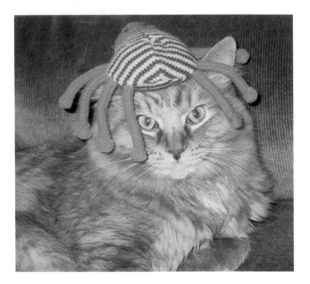

NAME: Isabella
AGE: 3
HOBBY: Playing with own hair

"If you want me in chaps,
it'll cost you another five
bucks."

NAME: Dusty
AGE: 3
HOBBY: Japanese pop

"This *is* my smile."

NAME: Chaz
AGE: 7
HOBBY: Taking you for
granted

"You're fired."

NAME: Donald
AGE: 9
HOBBY: Preening

"And they said smoking
crack was bad for me."

NAME: Precious
AGE: 3
HOBBY: Tearing open cereal
boxes

"What is it about our gang
colors you don't like?"

NAME: Franz
AGE: 5
HOBBY: Cooking with organ
meats

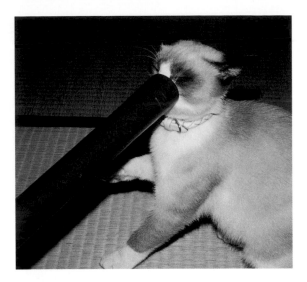

"Fritos, check. Twinkies, check. Bong hit, very check."

NAME: Wallace
AGE: 2
HOBBY: Tripping on the whole crazy universe

"Sure I believe in Santa Claus. Especially the meat on his legs."

NAME: Sludge
AGE: 2
HOBBY: Impressions of famous cats

"Now it's seventy-five trombones in the big parade."

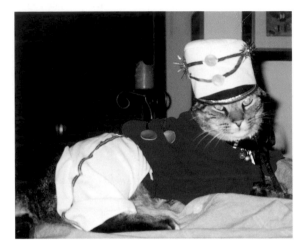

NAME: Gus
AGE: 8
HOBBY: Vegging out

"*Now* do you understand
why I prefer Hanukkah?"

NAME: Jenny
AGE: 1
HOBBY: Making dreidels out
of clay

"It's not too late to adopt,
you know."

NAME: Soba
AGE: 8
HOBBY: Writing haiku

"I'm not a bad ass. I have a bad ass."

NAME: Owsley
AGE: 4
HOBBY: Digging himself

"You'll stop laughing
when the rest of the
brotherhood gets here."

NAME: No. 616
AGE: 9
HOBBY: Marauding

"Thank you. We'll be here
all week. Try the veal."

NAME: Tony Braciole & His
Two Skeletons
AGE: 7
HOBBY: Craps

"Okay, who made the hash
brownies?"

NAME: Eve
AGE: 4
HOBBY: Alternative medicine

"How was I supposed to
know what's in a Long
Island Iced Tea?"

NAME: Chi-Chi
AGE: 3 months
HOBBY: Experimenting with
unknown substances

"Love to love you, baby."

NAME: Richie
AGE: 6
HOBBY: Cologne historian

"So that's the 'horizontal mambo.'"

NAME: Herschel
AGE: 9 months
HOBBY: Identity theft

"I know this hasn't ended
well for you, but I still
think we've had fun."

NAME: Puff
AGE: 10
HOBBY: Iyengar yoga

About the Author

Jim Edgar lives in Seattle, Washington. He is married with no children, or cats. He pays his bills by working for Microsoft Corporation as a software engineer.

If you enjoyed these bad cats, you will find many, many more at *www.mycathatesyou.com*.